Every New Day lies Within A Battle Field

LOUISE BRUFF

BookLeaf
Publishing

India | USA | UK

Presentation by BookLeaf Publishing

Web: www.bookleafpub.com

E-mail: info@bookleafpub.com

ISBN: 978-93-5744-315-9

First edition 2022

DEDICATION

To my long gone mother, three children and my
Grand-children

ACKNOWLEDGEMENT

I would like to express my greatest writing attributes of gratitude to my teachers, good friends, closest sisters, and family. who always encouraged my golden pen gift in writing and reading. There have been so many opportunities where I was able to inspire someone else through the wonderful writings I have created throughout the years.

Most importantly I want to acknowledge my butterfly friend who was gone too soon, memories held tight, I will forever cherish because she always motivated and helped contribute towards my skills and growth of my writing.

PREFACE

The motivation of these poem helped me to find myself, growing up as a young woman, and returning to the spot back home under a big coconut tree, lies a spot I marked that kept changing and evolving. A piece inside my heart continues to grow every time I reflect and begin to write. Writing these poems about my life taken place in a lot of places, with wounds and experiences as a young girl growing up allowed the help of being able to produce well- written stories or poems build my courage to grow along the pathways.

I grew to learn trusting myself to fight the battles of life kept my strong faith.
Even when life shows up like a storm and its rough, and seems like there will be no way out, I will never give up hope.

Life

Life begins with our feeling- how we feel,
what we do and what we think.
Life is our future reward for our past.

It is our minds that help us to understand others
and do things the way we feel they should be
done.

Let us do good to all people, especially those
who cannot help themselves. Let us not be
weary in doing for others when they need our
help. Let us help, respect and acknowledge the
natures of other, just as they are.

We interact by feelings. We do things the way in
which our spirits lead us.

Let us keep this knowledge with the strength of
our spirits.
Our feelings are the basis of our spiritual life.

Louise Bruff
1990

Learning to Live

In tone mist of a hungry Shadow the body fleas to survive. Over poverty downfalls everything in decay, from riches to rags a toned body is without food day to day. Oppression and hungry set him deep into temptation to play upon a glossing frame.

In the Crawling dry sandy land, the wild man discovers recovery from his shameless life his body stands. Encouraged to drink the bitter water and snatched into darkness and out from the light.

These two men rescued two sacks of fresh potatoes Shone eyebright. Warmth and fibre will fill the emptiness in the boat souls left from right.

A stone full stomach will grow no more, the stormy clouds will point their north. Anger proclaims its enemy, in the violence of fire and hunger for revenge. Are bare naked flesh fears with trembling emotions.

Every comfort Perished, as one laid in sorrow to burn in a furnace. One lied down and a red evil broke out from the under the land, while ones body moisten by the oils splat on his forbidden skin.

Blind eyes watched helplessly, whispering Words of faith and strength for one's new soul. Under the cloudy sky, minds strived vain glory but lowness. You could smell raiment mines bitter cry weary of his life. Their voices rolled with thunder like bees hovering in the den begging forgiveness. Buried in the heartland of life raindrops showed remorse on the parched bodies lying lifeless alone.

His body like a burning offering went down alive in a pity, under the wavy spark from the moonlight alone in the sky. Disappearing by the fire his eyes fell covered, blind in smoke like a baby calf in the glooming womb of its mother. No more words were left to be said but swelling words of vanity from the others. Roll over, roll over he fractured himself, tormented peeled like a potato did his skin peeled off, all nakedness wined.

2001

A Life Filled With Dreams

looking back life's learning is processed.
Everyone has a dream and with His grace, the
gates of life are open. We can finish where we
started yesterday no matter how old or young
one may be, or smart it is never too late to learn.
It is not where you start, it is how you finish.
There is no retirement in learning; stay young,
wait patiently and be fully born. Refire and
preserve hope of inspiration, challenge yourself.
You may be hit with a hammer and still rise
above. Look towards God for guidance
throughout the way, you must press on and be
bold. Remember You are the only one person to
carry on this dream. It is not failure that counts;
it is how much you put in. Always remain focus
on the bright light at the end of the tunnel. Let's
live in this dream of life.
 Louise Bruff 2015

The Drama of Life

After the thunderous rainfall had passed,
I witnessed the Beauty of the meadow lands and
realized how the changing seasons play an
intricate role in the cycle of life. I saw the
rainbows like decorations on a birthday present
hanging low in the open sky for all those to
see—A constant reminder that mankind is never
alone in the universe.

I watch the sky as ripples of sunlight fell to the
surface of the earth like golden dewdrops
silhouetted on green leaves. The rain refreshed
the earth and brought an abundance of tasty
earthworms from the ground for the hungry
birds to feed upon.

People and animals bathed in the beauty of the
sun that was scattered over the hills and trees.
After the thunderous rainfall had passed I saw
rainbows like islands of flowers dangling along
the way, moving gently to the rhythm of the
caring breeze.

I am marvelled have a great change of the
seasons and the loneliness of everything that
grows. I realize how the changing seasons play
an intricate role in the cycle of life's humanity
and being.

It makes me keen to listen and open up my eyes
to the loveliness and dream of it all.
It helps us understand life and my place in this
vast universe. But most of all, it makes me know
there is a greater power in charge of this great
universe. He gave us the earth for all its beauty
and majestic wonders .

Louise Bruff

2002

Spirit Divine

In a thirsty land, shadowed with wings fallen by a dragon's soul, it suffers for life.
Drunk in the wine of violence, the blend their bows and arrows. Aligned raged waves of a better gain, fighting to shoot away breath of pain.
Dumped in silent of sorrows, stirred tongues form like swords of bitter words. A dog return to face-to-face with its vomit. Afraid suddenly, the strict waves beneath the sea rolls and mourned with hostile blame.

Out of the land, chained under darkness the sea lion roared hungry smoke of pit pills and pillars. Drooling and clothed with garment hurt wounded casts down of a prisoners body laid to consume soil from the rain.

Out of the weakness the naked swine for revenge with forcing blood shielding among all. Shedding hope in the boundaries of dishonor, against each angry appointment. Sprung out of

the earth, souls were born on the island in the
battle.

Shaming the edge of the sword as the day of the
youth was shortened many souls a brave men
stood in vain. soon time will come to embrace.
A time to cast away, a time to hate all to heat all
weapons, wars and shameful ways. Once
reframed from embracing all within one braid a
single day, seemed living under a cluttered vile.

Louise Bruff
2011

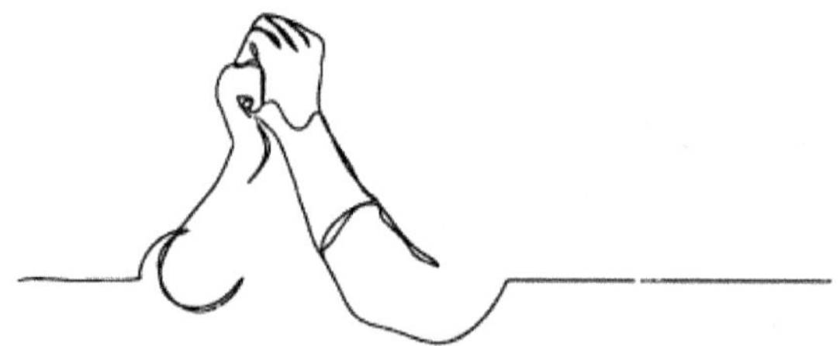

Out of The Dull Hill

As birds flew out the snares escaped.
Rivers of water run down against my face.
My life then sunk down to the ground.
The poor lives in poverty. As a shadow passes
over the ancient land, days of my elders are
broken by the gate of Grace.

Be nurtured as the plants growing stars of night.
Out of the broken and snares, a thirsty land is
thrown into a stony place then it is blinded by
my wounds in the deep gully.
Raise the poor from the stormy wind. Mountain
steps, hills and dry fields are removed from the
Rough sea, heaven been a beaten ancient
landmark.

Out of the dust our people brought low removed
the ancient landmark. In the red sea dull in the
dark as a stone in the deep water. Out the dust
the poor is still in poverty.
The wounded spirit is still broken, hungry
roaring in armour.
Days of the battle labour may not be rich to eat
the bread of sorrow flavour rather than gold.

Slant before the ancient's land might be a strong
city to escape, just like as birds out the broken
snares. A cry by the sea speaks more by night by
a pillars fire blueness of the wounded poor edge
of the world.

Louise Bruff
Feb 2016

Love Hurts

Love is what hurts us
and that what enslaves our thoughts like a
stranger to our own brother land.
Love is to be the road of letters driven, to be
trampled under the foot, love is like a dog
roaming searching for food and growing to find
shaft on their wings.
Love is what makes us bleed inside. Love is like
pride worn royal gold. Love is casting down and
only a fool would believe in that love is like a
crushing thunder, rolling, or heavy a rain cloud
pouring down.

A beaten child would cling to the fist of as the
beaten wife strikes with blindness telling lies to
the police. Love is to forgive and understand and
sometimes to walk away, for only a slave stays a
victim. For love is a trial, sitting in darkness, a
poison with broken hearts of suffering.
A thirsty sore, burnt out of fire for love leaves a
heavy or healthy heart week upon a deserted
island. Love is a tree understood, rooted and
tasteless with no water or branches, will form
striped and weak, almost one's deepest misery.

Loved heart laid s ripped on the gravel, each
scrape and wounds remind me to lift myself of
the rocky ground.

The table of my heart pours out water from the
milky skies, subtle of my heart well then rises
above. The one the snare is broken from a loving
war that continues to prosper, so wholesome
with purity.

Louise Bruff
2011

Never Give Up

I never gave up on hope; I am the woman in the
belly of the wrecked ship, where I lost my
identity and love ones.
Shocked enslaved by in my bondage torn away
from the one and all. Hungry and angry sold like
a feast and labour like a beast. I crawled alone
with no garments to cover my sores beneath feet.
Forward, I continue to move with the spirit of
the blue mountain breeze. Thirsty, tormented
darkness of the scorpions naked I seen my
shame and confiscated my pride; an empty
vessel titter- tottering upon raging seas.

Down the hills and over the mountains like an
eagle flying in unbearable restraints. Out into the
light full of glory the songs of the brave bird
carried and healed my holy soul, whispering
sweet words of wisdom. An ongoing help filled
me up.

The search is to find clean water to drink or
food, embracing abundantly my greedy soul of
that which I may never go hungry again. I have
not yet reached my destination; I will not give
up bringing my future up oh so big, mighty and
strong. Driving a monster out from the sea is one
that keeps me free to strive, to stand for tall like
a solid rock or a beak new tree.

2011
Louise Bruff

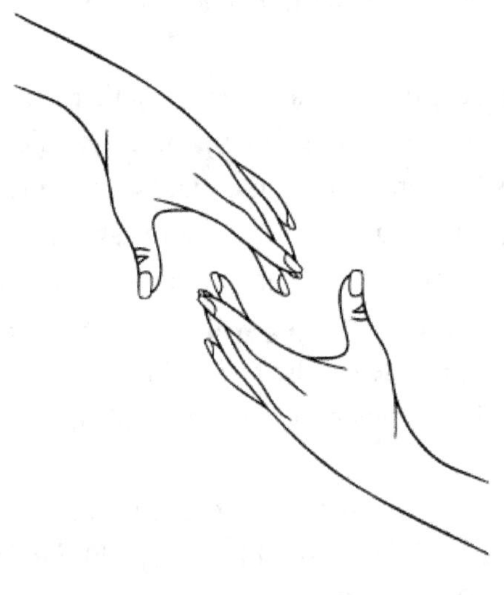

The Mother of Children

His prediction was to be a son of your womb, but black youth he was forced into. 17 years old gone down into the streets, the many crying faces of many tears fell under the cloudy dark sky.

Mothers, grandmothers, sisters, father, and grandfathers, among other people who didn't know him protestant shouting, "seven times bang, bang, bang!" in front of the store. As a mother I could feel pain buried in my heart, wounded in everything within me the souls of my people grieved the fruits of human love and truth flaunts when the sun goes down.

Love is cursed in our hearts and we are suffering. The breath of life is fought with a battle. Between the suns, moon, and stars hovering above the city everything grew darker and flame on the land.

A city that is divided by red seas and was beaten by the yoke in hunger and blind from the hatred.

The soul of my people are the divine suppliers to
our motherland. The body and blood of the
youth is lying in the street. The womb of the
morning weeping for answers from the mountain
in skies deep Valley. Sing in the morning earth
sing without crying. We are all human and just
like a colourful rainbow, we are one blood. We
are voices of many waters thunderous in the
streets of blood. The hardness of these men's
hearts will weigh us down, the weapon of feast
is killed before each youth's future.

I never will forget summer heat of the year 2013
and mother treasure plenty of talking and plenty
of crying. I watch TV and read the newspaper.
Even I didn't know him. I see tears in the
mother's eyes I could also feel the pain. I was a
mother to there was nothing less left but to feel
the pain.

Louise Bruff
February 2016

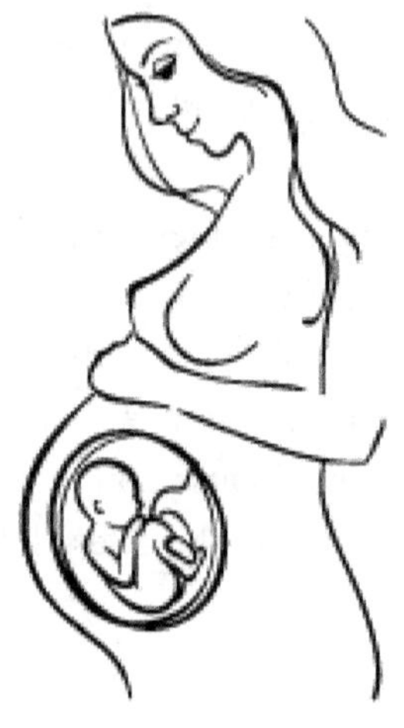

The Land I Remember

The place where I was born and grew up, I
remember well.
I would get up early in the morning just to see
the glowing of the sun in the open sky. I would
watch the morning light spread out like a heavy
curtain over the hills and into the deep valley.

I remember the sweet smell of flowers in the
early morning, the flowers with Dewey leaves
waving and dancing in the cool morning breeze.

I remember the feeling of wet grass on my bare
feet, the sunshine stepping across my face.
I remember the luscious mango tree that
surrounded the house. Sitting under the big
mango tree, inhaling the distinct still smell of
succulent fruits, the taste of mangos like honey
in my mouth, their colour like ripples of
sunshine; or climbing up into the trees like a big
bird, eating the mangos to the seed.

I remember the butterflies moving through the crushed grass and over the heads of the wild shrubs. I remember the big trees fluttering in the warm summer air and the birds singing sweet songs. As the evening drew near, I saw birds with graceful wings stretched across the valley like a weaving banner, singing hymns, this is my father's world.

Louise Bruff
2016

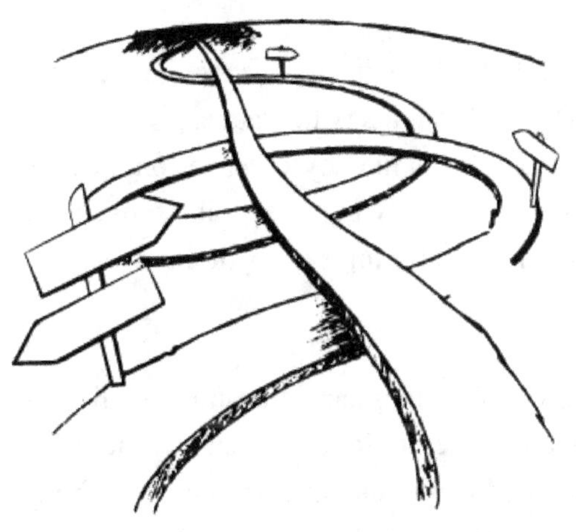

On The Wings Of The Dawn

In the early morning, the clear blue sky comes overhead. The morning skylights of like a fountain of life fill in the house, and the hushing day breeze sweeps above the heavenly heights. The gleaming sunlight scatters over the fields and forest trees.

The sunlight sheds it's beams around me. It's girding my thoughts with gladness.
My mind dances like joyful leaves on the trees that whispers softly in my ear, like spoken words unfolding sweet tidings of joy to my weary being.

The swirling leaves carry blissful melodies to my wanting heart. For a moment, I watched the silhouetted leaves dancing upon me, touching my face, making me giggle. The delicate leaves take on a new meaning, transforming in to A bright glow of orange gold like the rising of the morning sun.

My heart awakens with steadfastness, vitality
and contentment. I guess with wonder at the
invitation to love nature and embrace the beauty
and tranquillity of each passing day.

Louise Bruff
2003

My Hero

You haven't forgotten for you are my hero,
when I think of vision you were laying down in
a hiding place.
Your vision is full in my eyes. You are the great
rain of the sky, living in the dust of the earth. I
learned that I am becoming. The rain was my
strength and a shield from shame of the
yesterday. I can't change now! I am all beat up.

As servants of the field hold mercy from being
brought forth with no peace of love. You are
found of no privileges in the land. As your eyes
closed the darkness came on. Climbing an
avalanche deep or buried low valleys to hide. I
escaped out from the lion's paw, scurried past the
sheep's in the wilderness. The poor Of my
people that all the battle through pathways to
freedom as people were pulled out the net. No
labour of love in the sky went showers down
teardrops in fears from yesterday of the
struggling war. As you reach out your hands to
the world, and no one embraces you. Your goal
is striving to live and survive as we all just want
to live the life.

Louise Bruff
2008

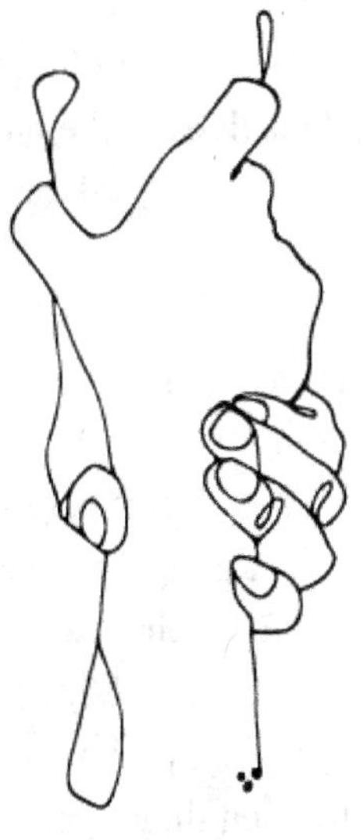

The Troubled World

The world is full of tribulation and woes. So many man-made weapons are tearing the world and its people apart. My earthly sight is limited, and so is our children's future. I can't see. I am troubled when I consider the forgotten children who have lost their lives in the burning fires of war, or who have gone to bed hungry, crying out for food.

It brings tears to my weary eyes. I feel like a broken vessel being tossed a bowl on the raging sea. My grieving heart feels sore within me each given day. I can just imagine the children's voices crying out for their lives, men and women bawling for their freedom. My soul is weeping, anxious heart is crying, moaning out to the world leaders to open their eyes to help bring freedom, peace and hope, and to heed the children's cries and relieve the pains they are suffering. Too many children have lost their lives and their homes have gotten dismantled by war.

Sometimes they have ended up on the streets. They have no place to call home, and because of this, they rebel. Our children are hurting and nations are fighting against each other while others are at play. Whenever, I read the newspapers and watch TV, it gives me an image of what is happening around the world. People all around a wounded and dying by the thousands every given day.

The world needs people with earthly love in their hearts, a love that will transform every heart and make us into new creatures of the earth, that will help us to be always kind and loving towards other people, that through His divine love will bind us together; that will stop us from fighting against one another, and wipe out hatred.
Also, the world needs people of good heart and goodwill, working together, people with good community mindfulness to build strong leaders, that will help us live and get a long each day.

Today we hear people talk about social change, but no one seems to do much about the conflict of war that surrounds the world and its people. What solution is necessary to resolve this matter? My dreams hope to see an end to all weapons of mass destruction. My heart will be glad to see all chemical weapons wiped out. Maybe a result, the Lives of many children and wet women will be speared and people will live in a healthy world.

No weapons of mass destruction should stand over the children and violence stand over our children. As death unfolds its wings, I long to see the world filled with people living in an abundance of freedom, peace, love, and tolerance.

Louise Bruff
2002

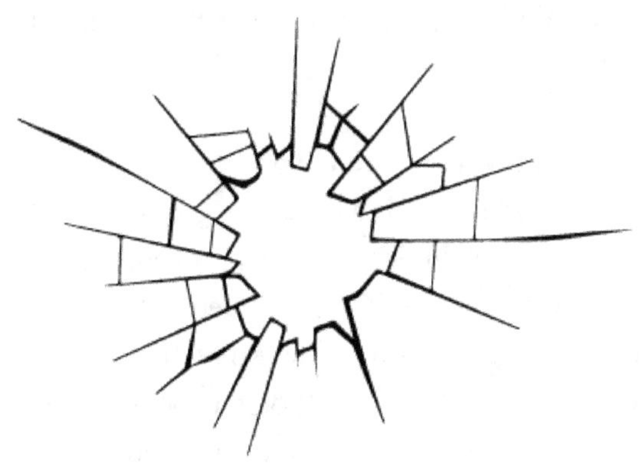

Life Is A Lottery

For first foremost you don't get to choose who
your parents are.
You don't get to choose where and when you
were born.
Nor do you get a chance to get to choose
education you want.
Especially if you don't have the money and the
opportunity.

So, what do you get to choose?
Getting older, looking back, I began to focus
more on what choices I made as a young girl, I
wanted to stay in school. I wanted to travel. In
my imagination I saw myself traveling the
world. When I was 17, I thought about the
country of Canada. I had relatives there some of
them had moved back home both men and
women. Some relative stayed in Canada and
some of my teenage friends who also have been
schoolmates. I hoped to go back to school and
work. In those days that was hardly possible. In
fact it was really a party time for many of them!

We didn't choose get to choose what we look like and how you address ourselves.

My mother was fine with leaving but my father didn't share his thoughts about her leaving. So, coming to Canada was my first serious choice in travelling. The question of course, as did I regret it?

No, although it didn't live up to my dreams I'm still here, and life goes on. You can look back and wonder if you had the power or an opportunity to change some things you have done you would've done so many things differently.

Taking big chances didn't seem possible, was it? In many ways you can't back time, nor return home because home has now changed, and on a better note so have you. The best thing in our lives are our children because they have the ability to change your life forever. Trying to go to school and working a part-time job not to mention looking at the family changes the perspective of life. Some people can do it but not very many. Perhaps, something has to give. There are days that one doesn't want to look back on. Days of being insulted and ignored or having no way to fight back. I'm glad my children are living in a world they are able to fight back, standing their ground. Fighting more with strength and with heads held up higher than mine. When you look back at all yesterday, I think if I had the chance, the power and the choice, my life would have been different. I would have more financial freedom and I would have a well-paid good job in a great place. people around me would then see me differently and treat me differently, like someone who just won the lottery of life.

Louise Bruff
2000

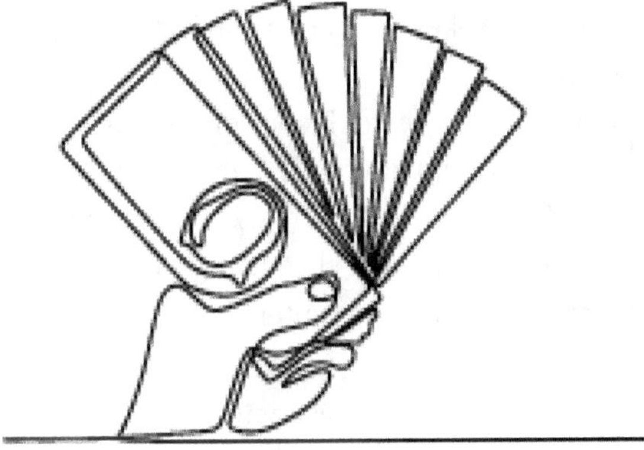

Moonshine for Glory

All the lanes are shut down, no lane available to travel. The world is watching. We are not being kind to one another.
We are guilty of shame for yesterdays and pain or sorrow has blinded and damaged our souls.
Are we to say sorry?
Our soul is broken and he is waiting for the changed.
let our voices be heard. let our freedom be granted among all multitude. Are we to be blame? We are being kind to others. I beg you to cease if the violence of change upon us.
Humanity is crumbling, falling like dust.

On the ground, on our doorstep are mirrors, the world is watching, the world is watching.

Yet we are all called humans, so when will the world open their eyes to see the trueness. The world will riddle under attack if my people never heard not his voice, out of the darkness unchained of violence has risen onto darkness of morning. The cries in vain for peace.

The river streams ocean weeps deeply as shadow
encompasses the world. So wounded by cruel
acts young vines are cut off. We are just human,
families and neighbours and in crisis mother of
the children, daughters, sisters, aunts, brothers'
fathers bruised, crushed in the flames. Ashes of
dust entrances grievous morning of sadness.
Human blood stain on the dry land. People are
dying in the street. Great start falling onto
bottomless pit the ocean rice, human cries and
more and the thunder roar.
Take a look at the man in the moon. He holds
my future for tomorrow. His message; he is in
the diminished land. The creatures are perishing
in the grass, plants are dry, doll and withered.
Away comes no new hope for a new beginning.
All lanes shut down people groan. No lane to
walk on the Kings Highway. Are we here to take
responsibility for our actions? Are we here to
blame?
The world is watching, the world is waiting and
it awaits change, the choice is ours.

Louise Bruff
2000

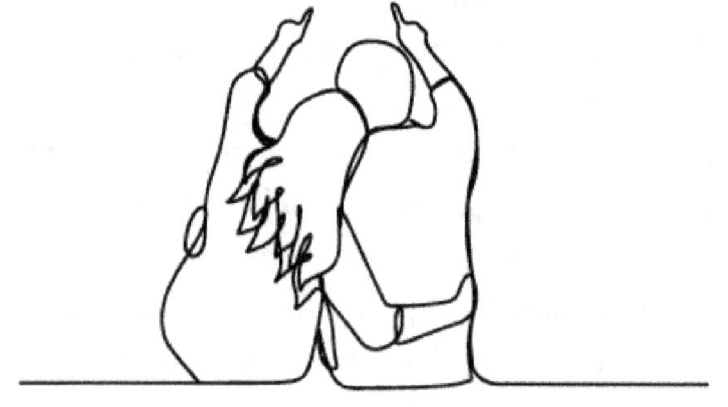

Hope

Some mornings can be rainy and gloomy
sometimes when the rain stops falling like tears
from the sky and the sun comes shining out it is
such a glorious state. As a new day breaks
through the clearing sky and a gleam of sunlight
shines on the wetland as the sun begins to rise,
the clouds wander away like leaves for
frolicking in this autumn breeze. As a Morning
dans a glimpse of hope appears to the story
heavens the moon hides under today's time sky
the sunshine's each day bringing joy, health,
beauty and brilliance for everyone to cherish and
embrace joy comes out in the morning.

Louise Bruff
2000

In His Glorious Presence

In the glory of his presence, we bow.
For we are His people, the fruit of light, grace,
the seeds of the land and the salt of the earth.
In the beauty of his holiness, we lie basking in
his grace. For his people shall Florissant flourish
and grow, fashioning the land from their very
essence, the likeness of God.

A land that he promised to a chosen few if they
would obey and acknowledge Him in every way
by His grace his shall add salt and flavour to the
blessed land, a salt that shall never lose it savour.

My heart is forever longing, thirsting for that
land I dream about, and its fervent expectancy,
that constant yearning for a better place, a better
time, that transfigures is my soul through space
and time.

Then into the great beyond, where the wonder of
his majesty is made manifest, the land burst
forth with joy. The Saints from every race, the
chosen few, find sweet peace, love and
tranquillity there.

Louise Bruff
2002

Prayer

In my life,
when doubts and fears provoke me,
teach me the way of faithfulness and lead me on
a bright and heavenly journey.

Whenever I am confronted by despair, the joy of
your love uplifts my spirits. When perils come to
test my faith, you teach me the way to be brave
and replace my heart ache with songs of joy.

In my life Whenever I am way down with oils
and struggles, you build your hedges around me.
Oh God, teach me to know you're willing to say
that you're will is dying to be done.
Lead me to your divine light, grant me the
grease and console my heart, and to ease my
fears. Take away every bird and that may slow
me down on my journey into your arms.

Just as a shining light that progresses, shining
brighter and brighter onto a perfect day, preserve
my life each day from the stress. Save me now.

Louise Bruff

The place Where I Would Set Down And Gather My Thoughts

My favourite place where I would gather my thoughts was on a little hillside surrounded by trees overlooking the running stream that cut across the flat land. Sometimes, at twilight, when the heavy rain fell and the stream swelled, the water flowed like a wide river among the twisted rocks and twisted thorns.

My closest thoughts would surround my heart and my mind. The thing that gave my peace and security of mind was to sit on that hillside like a shepherd watching over his flock waiting for a splendid light or guiding star to brighten the way through the darkness of the night.

In my mind's eyes, I saw a crowd of children sitting in the open field near a little hillside. I stared Intently at the night sky, hoping to see at any passing moment, some glorious light in the open sky, filling them with great joy and youthful Bliss.

Sometimes I would stand up on the little hillside with my head bowed and my eyes closed when I felt my body moved, I would open my eyes. I would raise up my head looking towards the open sky, which was clear as crystal. I saw billions of stars both small and great stretching across the night sky in a never-ending sea.

The stars seem so bright in fair in their heavenly heights. I wanted to count the stars, but they were numberless. In the silence of the night, I gazed and I gazed until I found myself singing songs and smiling at the beautiful stars that shone in the warmth of the night.

The stars were so clear and so near to my sight. I wanted to reach out with my hands to touch them all. In the vision of the night, I saw the shining stars. They seemed so alive, like a multitude of little angel spreading the graceful wings in majestic flight across the milky way.

Which triumphant smile, I rejoiced at the stars
that shone in the heavenly heights, unreachable
to my human capacity. For a brief moment, a
spirit of understanding and deep knowledge
came over my inner being within inexplicable
calm, Beauty and brilliance in the dark of night
to where people travel throughout the universe
waiting on the starlight night to confirm what
the Las Olas looking for a guiding hand.

Louise Bruff
2000

Life Goes On

Gone too soon.
Memories hold tight onto hurts to touch and share as a reminder of her sweet presence is still here.

Remember this little flower you brought into the world. She was the tree of your life as you steered to the left avoiding all fears.

In the womb, love until morning dew. The fruit of love, blooms like August in June and how joyful of the little branches which grew into beautiful flowers like the sun and the moon. Remember her sweet voice and laughter, smile and jokes as a ripple across the clear blue sky. I just want you to know these memories, cherish them! As they speak to the human soul. They are written on the table of the human heart but said with a golden spoon. They are powerful. In all honors, you have the power within you.

Embrace the table of your own heart. You must
put them together between the strings of a harp;
like a music there is giggling, as kisses are
laying in the deep in and heavily sky for days on
millions. Stretching across the ocean is a bed of
clouds singing songs for you. You are not alone.
No weeping no worry my friend, for you are not
alone.

Those tears will come in the morning, but they
dry up under the sunlight.

Smiles will come again when the birds are
singing praises. You are not alone. Don't be
afraid. Your gift of strength is like a mountain.
Your gift of strength is like a mountain!

Louise Bruff
2000

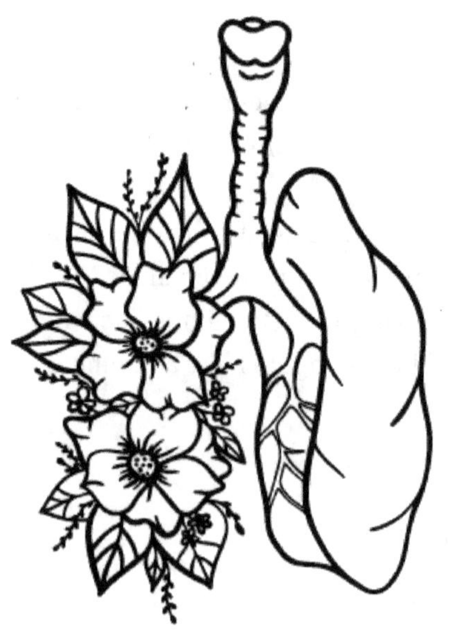